*The Onesimus Workshop*

# the ONESIMUS workshop

## Welcoming Former Prisoners into the Life of the Church

*Rev. Don Allsman*
*Cathy Allsman, M.A.*

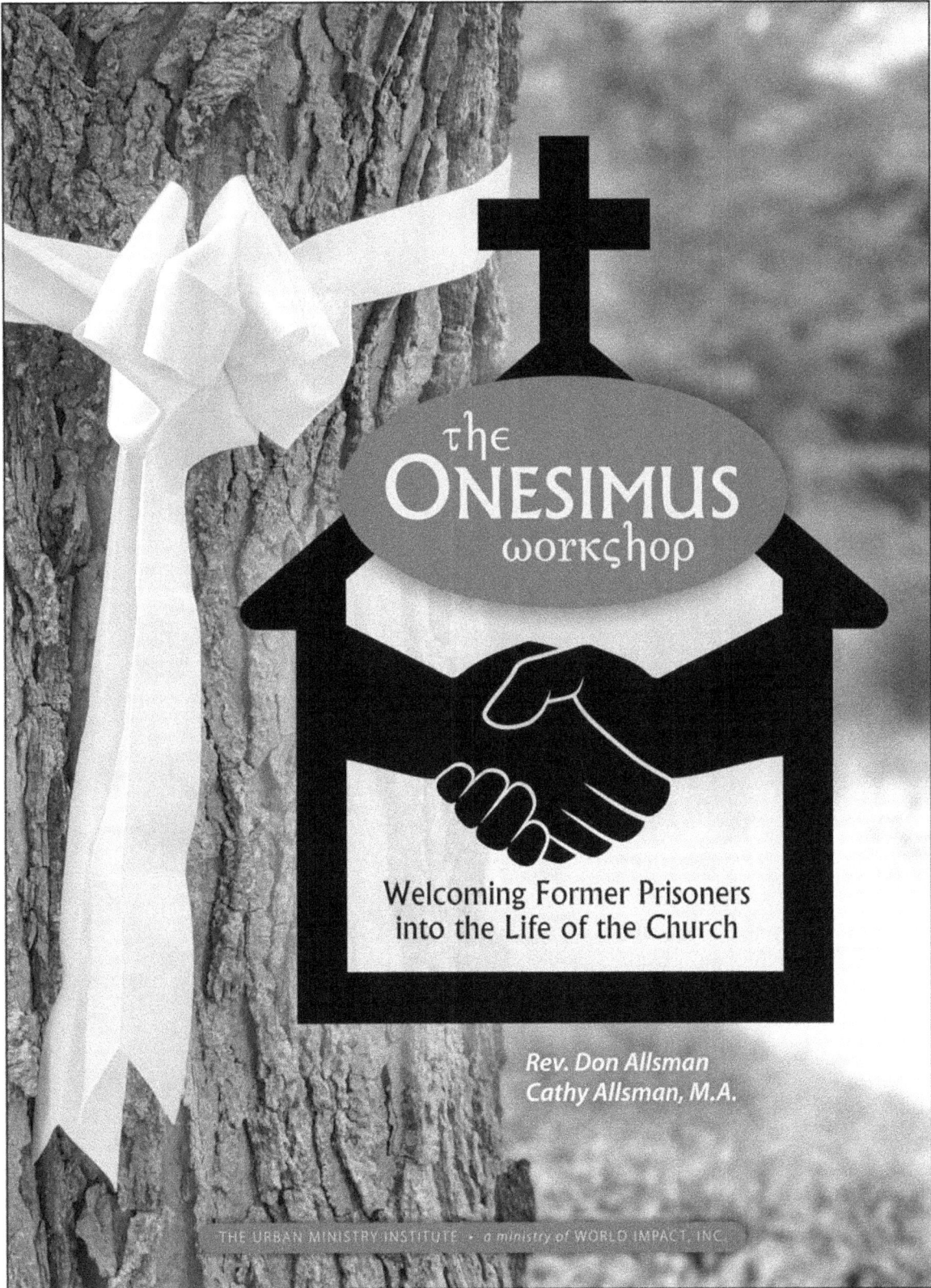

THE URBAN MINISTRY INSTITUTE · a ministry of WORLD IMPACT, INC.

TUMI Press
3701 East 13th Street North
Wichita, Kansas 67208

*The Onesimus Workshop: Welcoming Former Prisoners into the Life of the Church*
*Participant Workbook*

© 2018. The Urban Ministry Institute. All Rights Reserved. Copying, redistribution, and/or sale of these materials, or any unauthorized transmission, except as may be expressly permitted by the 1976 Copyright Act or in writing from the publisher is prohibited. Requests for permission should be addressed in writing to:

The Urban Ministry Institute
3701 East 13th Street North
Wichita, KS 67208

ISBN: 978-1-62932-510-1

Published by TUMI Press
A division of World Impact, Inc.

The Urban Ministry Institute is a ministry of World Impact, Inc.

To current and former TUMI students in prison.
You are among the most gifted, fearless, and dedicated warriors
for Christ and his Kingdom that we have ever known.
You have inspired us to work even harder to
raise up leaders for his harvest fields.

## About the Authors

Rev. Don Allsman served as Vice President of World Impact for twenty-seven years, and as the Executive Director of Satellite Ministries for The Urban Ministry Institute (TUMI) from 2006-2018. He earned a Bachelor of Science degree in Industrial Engineering at California State University – Fresno and a Master of Business Administration from Wichita State University. Don has written several books that are used as textbooks for TUMI's program: *The Heroic Venture: A Parable of Project Leadership* (2006), *Jesus Cropped from the Picture: Why Christians Get Bored and How to Renew Them to Vibrant Faith* (2010), *Think Again: Transformation That Yields a Return on God's Investment* (2018), and a book co-written with Dr. Don Davis: *Fight the Good Fight of Faith: Playing Your Part in God's Unfolding Drama* (2015).

Cathy Allsman served as Incarceration Ministries Specialist for The Urban Ministry Institute from 2012-2018. Cathy was responsible to oversee dozens of TUMI sites in prisons across the country, serving hundreds of students. Prior to that role, she was World Impact's Candidate Services Coordinator, reviewing missionary applications and counseling potential applicants about joining World Impact as a missionary. Cathy graduated from Wichita State University with an MA in Communicative Disorders, specializing in Audiology. As a Research Audiologist for the House Ear Institute she served as liaison between the research and clinical departments, contributing to cutting-edge advancement in hearing aid technology in the 1980s. Cathy and Don have two sons, Ryan and Mark, and a daughter-in-law, Janée.

Now the Allsmans are a part of Completion Global, Inc., a ministry dedicated to mobilizing the Church to its kingdom purpose.

## Table of Contents

## Foreword

One of the great untapped pools of human capital in America and around the world are the prison populations alongside those who were formerly incarcerated. The heart of the Christian Gospel is the conviction that anyone can be transformed by the love of God, the grace of our Lord Jesus Christ, and the renewing power of the Holy Spirit. The God and Father of our Lord Jesus is a God of the impossible, who can turn a prisoner-on-the-run, Onesimus ("useful"), into a fruitful, effective companion of the great Apostle Paul. God is not limited to personal histories, scientific data charts, professional assessments, or existential probabilities. God transcends what seems possible, infuses it with his own wisdom and grace, and transforms human situations and hearts to glorify his own great name. Plainly stated, God can do anything. And this conviction, that God is the God of the broken and the discarded, undergirds the wisdom and discernment of this fine workbook, the product of Don and Cathy Allsman's deep spiritual vision and practically wise approach.

As our most experienced colleagues in making disciples among those who have been formerly incarcerated, Don and Cathy have given extensive time, investment, and reflection to the thorny issues surrounding the potential challenges and rich opportunities of making disciples among those within the Church-on-the-inside and those who have been released. Their care and wisdom make this workshop an invaluable resource for all who are interested in discerning a kingdom response to the ministry to the incarcerated. For the cynic, this workbook will demonstrate a deep faith in the power of God to change and transform the prisoner, and for the fearful, you will find a clear, wise approach to avoiding naive, Pollyannaish approaches to discipling the formerly incarcerated. And, for the congregations and believers who desire to make a difference for the Kingdom in deeply impacting the lives and families of former prisoners, this booklet will prove to be a treasure. Filled with good theology, practical wisdom, and smart advice for individuals and congregations ministering in a jail or prison, this work will soon become one of their go-to texts to help them do good ministry to the Church-inside-the-walls.

As those whom I count as my close personal friends, I see this insightful text as an extension of the Allsmans' generous hearts and critical minds. May all who read this apply its principles and lessons. I believe if we do, we may see genuine transformation occur, not only in many jails and prisons around the nation, but also in the lives and ministries of hundreds of biblical churches who are willing to respond to the Savior's call to serve the unlovely and the least of these, those with whom he still identifies today.

Dr. Don L. Davis
Wichita, Kansas
June 6, 2018

## Acknowledgments

Thanks to the dozens of former prisoners and prison ministers across America who participated in focus groups to shape this workshop. Thanks to Paul Chan for helping us shape this vision.

## Introduction

Welcome to the Onesimus Workshop!

The purpose of the Onesimus Workshop is to orient churches to the process of welcoming former prisoners into the life of their church for building up the body of Christ. Our vision is to equip you with the beginning steps toward effectively incorporating former prisoners into your church community. We cannot equip you with everything you will need along the way – you will have to learn that through experience and dependence on the Holy Spirit. But we do hope to get you started down this exciting journey.

We believe that revival can come to the churches of America through seminary-trained, eager, and talented men and women who have endured the hardships of prison life. They are ready to come back to communities where they were once a liability, in order to bring the redemption they have experienced through the Gospel of Jesus Christ.

When World Impact began in 1971, teaching children's Bible clubs in the inner city, we did not have prisoners on our minds. But as our ministry grew, and we started working with adults, planting churches, and providing leadership training, God led us into equipping the incarcerated. Now, we have over 1,400 current students inside the walls, and several hundred more who have been released with seminary education.

We have been eager to help them get plugged into churches upon release, but we discovered that it is difficult for them to make the transition from prison to civilian life. This led us to an examination of how to train churches to welcome former prisoners into their communities. That is the basis for the Onesimus Workshop.

We want to see your church strengthened by incorporating members who use their gifts as redeemed ambassadors of Christ.

The name "Onesimus" comes from the book of Philemon. Paul wrote Philemon as a letter about Onesimus, Philemon's runaway slave whom Paul had taken in and found to be an asset in ministry. He wrote that "formerly he was useless to you, but now he has become useful both to you and to me" (Philem. 11, NIV). Like the prisoners of today,

Onesimus was not highly valued by worldly standards, but Paul found him useful, just like former prisoners can be today.

This workshop is designed to help you get started. We can show you the way. But you will need to do the work. This is an opportunity of a lifetime. God bless you as you consider his will for your church.

# *The Onesimus Vision*

## Objectives

- Understand the background for the formation of the Onesimus vision.

- Appreciate the powerful effects of cultural differences.

- Recognize the amazing opportunity for your church to have trained, zealous leaders.

## Content

### I. The History of World Impact and The Urban Ministry Institute (TUMI)

A.  C1, C2, C3 paradigm

### *Interaction of Class, Culture, and Race*

*(Rev. Dr. Don L. Davis)*

*See full chart in Appendix 10: Interaction of Class, Culture, and Race.*

**African-American**

**Asian**

$C_1$

$C_1$

$C_2$

$C_2$

**Major Cultural Indicators:**
- Where they live
- Where they work
- Where educated

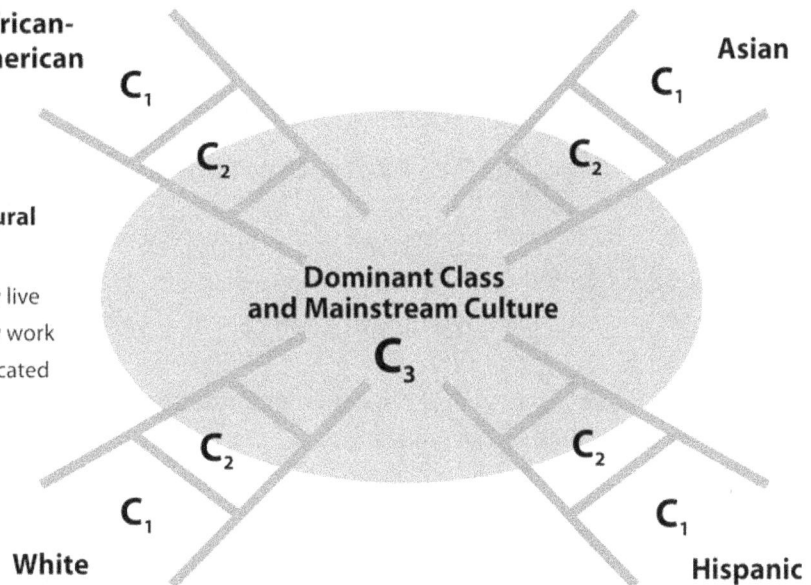

**Dominant Class and Mainstream Culture**

$C_3$

$C_2$

$C_2$

$C_1$

$C_1$

**White**

**Hispanic**

*See full chart in
Appendix 11:
Authentic Freedom
in Jesus Christ.*

**Biblical Precedence (Acts 15)**
*(Rev. Dr. Don L. Davis)*

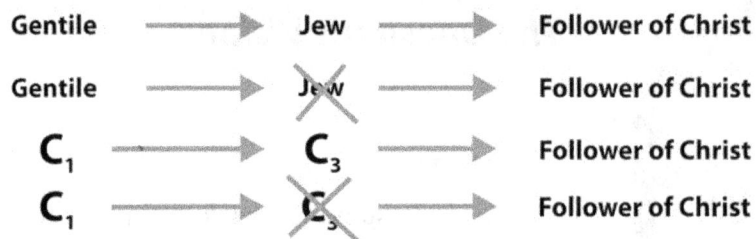

| Gentile | ⟶ | Jew | ⟶ | Follower of Christ |
| Gentile | ⟶ | ~~Jew~~ | ⟶ | Follower of Christ |
| $C_1$ | ⟶ | $C_3$ | ⟶ | Follower of Christ |
| $C_1$ | ⟶ | ~~$C_3$~~ | ⟶ | Follower of Christ |

B.  The Urban Ministry Institute (TUMI)

C.  TUMI in prisons

## II. Background of the Onesimus Workshop

A.  *The purpose of the Onesimus Workshop is to orient churches to the process of welcoming former prisoners into the life of their church for building up the body of Christ.*

B.  The name "Onesimus" comes from the book of Philemon: "formerly he was useless to you, but now he has become useful both to you and to me" (Philem. 11, NIV).

## III. Two Approaches to Reentry

A.  Therapeutic Approach

B.  Identity Approach

C.  What former prisoners need more than anything is a *group of friends*

| Our Experience with the Incarcerated: Approaches to Effective Transformation | | |
|---|---|---|
| | **Therapeutic Approach** | **Identity Approach** |
| Starts with | Individual (internal) | Kingdom of God (external) |
| Pursuing | Felt needs-actualization | Cosmic purpose |
| Objective | Break destructive cycles | Identity subsumed (whole) |
| Solution | Find, accept, love self | Freedom from self-preoccupation |
| Primary Goals | Families; recidivism | Vision for ministry (all dimensions) |
| Secondary Goals | Personal holiness | Families; recidivism |
| Means | Job, housing, programs | Friends, community, internship |

## IV. The Opportunity of a Lifetime

A. Seminary-trained, zealous leaders bringing their gifts and abilities to your church

B. 2 Timothy 2.2 (ESV) : ". . . and what you [Timothy] have heard from me [Paul] in the presence of many witnesses entrust to faithful men [Onesimus], who will be able to teach others also."

C.  The Yellow Ribbon[1]

*I'm comin' home, I've done my time.*
*Now I've got to know what is and isn't mine.*
*If you received my letter telling you I'd soon be free,*
*Then you'll know just what to do, if you still want me.*

*Tie a yellow ribbon 'round the ole oak tree.*
*It's been three long years, do you still want me?*
*If I don't see a ribbon 'round the ole oak tree,*
*I'll stay on the bus, forget about us, put the blame on me.*
*If I don't see a yellow ribbon 'round the ole oak tree.*

*Bus driver, please look for me,*
*Because I couldn't bear to see what I might see.*
*I'm really still in prison, and my love, she holds the key.*
*A simple yellow ribbon's what I need to set me free.*

*Tie a yellow ribbon 'round the ole oak tree.*
*It's been three long years, do you still want me?*
*If I don't see a ribbon 'round the ole oak tree,*
*I'll stay on the bus, forget about us, put the blame on me.*
*If I don't see a yellow ribbon 'round the ole oak tree.*

## Summary of This Session

- World Impact developed The Urban Ministry Institute to train leaders that extended to training prisoners.

- Local churches can benefit from incorporating seminary-trained former prisoners into their communities upon release from prison.

- It will take effort to welcome them into your church.

## In the Next Session We Will Seek To:

- Acknowledge your fears and appreciate fears that prisoners have.

- Understand what prisoners experience that is different from civilian life.

- Recognize the factors that lead to recidivism.

---

1   "Tie a Yellow Ribbon Round the Ole Oak Tree" (Levine and Brown, 1973).

**Questions for Discussion**

- What did you learn about cultural differences that you didn't know or appreciate before?
- What makes you excited about the Onesimus Workshop?
- What makes you concerned or fearful about the Onesimus Workshop?

# Understanding Prison Culture

## In the Last Session We Attempted To:
- Understand the background for the formation of the Onesimus vision.
- Appreciate the powerful effects of cultural differences.
- Recognize the amazing opportunity for your church to have trained, zealous leaders.

## Objectives of This Session:
- Acknowledge your fears and appreciate fears that prisoners have.
- Understand what prisoners experience that is different from civilian life.
- Recognize the factors that lead to recidivism.

## Content

### I.  Be Candid about Your Hopes and Fears.

A.  Committing crimes upon their release

B.  Victim of crime

C.  Source of hope

D.  Unsavory element to the church

E.  Adding another burden to the church

F.  Overwhelm the church budget

G.  Prey upon the good-hearted servants in the church

H.  Start well but end in failure

## II. Acknowledge the Hopes and Fears That Former Prisoners Have.

A.  Never receive acceptance by other Christians

B.  Don't know how to find a church on the outside

C.  Won't find the same level of support as on the inside

D.  Never have the same level of responsibility that they have inside prison

E.  Might not make it on the outside

F.  Pressure to make up for lost time

G.  Temptations they've never faced may overwhelm them

H.  Being alone, rejected, and sent back to prison

## III. Culture of Prison

The dictionary defines institutionalization as "lacking the will or ability to think and act independently because of spending a long time in an institution." Prisoners worry about becoming institutionalized, but they are caught in a double bind. If they DON'T adapt to prison culture, they probably won't survive very well. If they DO adapt to prison culture, they risk becoming more and more institutionalized as time goes on. In the prison environment there is too much idle time and few opportunities for independent thinking. Almost all prisoners become institutionalized to a certain degree within 18-24 months. Inmate culture, for the most part, is anti-social. It promotes fear, dishonesty, self-centeredness, and aggression. The longer a person is incarcerated, the more he or she is hardened by exposure to prison culture.[1]

A.  Decision-making skills atrophy

B.  Need for constant vigilance

C.  Constant interaction

D.  Direct and intense communication

---

1    Prison Fellowship Online Training Module "Prison Culture: A Prisoner's World," 2012.

   E.  Worship services are different

   F.  Bartering economy

   G.  Persistent shame, disappointment and loss

   H.  Dehumanizing environment

   I.  The meaning of tattoos is different

## IV. Shifting to Civilian Life

   A.  Adjusting to no longer keeping constant vigilance

   B.  Desperation to make up for lost time

   C.  New-found freedom can be overwhelming

   D.  Loss of brotherhood

   E.  Racial and gender segregation

   F.  Moving back home

   G.  Unrealistic expectations

## V. Criminogenic Factors[2]

   A.  Beliefs

   B.  Peers

   C.  Personality

   D.  Family dysfunction

---

2  https://www.prisonfellowship.org/resources/training-resources/in-prison/on-going-ministry/criminogenic-needs-risk-returning-prison/?utm_source=NEWS&utm_medium=EMAIL&utm_campaign=PF-AWR&utm_term=NEWS&utm_content=risks%20of%20recidivism&spMailingID=17753810&spUserID=MTI0MjkyMzYwNzk0S0&spJobID=1062106038&spReportId=MTA2MjEwNjAzOAS2

E.  Low self-control

F.  Substance abuse

## VI. The Difference Between Jails and Prisons

A.  Jails

B.  Prisons

## Summary of This Session

- Church members and prisoners have hopes and fears.
- Prisoners incarcerated for 18 months become enculturated into prison culture.
- Prisoners need a community of friends to help them re-enculturate from prison culture to civilian culture or they are likely to re-offend and go back to prison.

## In the Next Session We Will Seek To:

- Understand the time and effort it will take to help a former prisoner adapt.
- Recognize the differences between a systemic approach and a programmatic approach.
- Appreciate the seven keys that will make the process successful.

## Questions for Discussion

- After hearing what it is like in prison, why might it be hard for a former prisoner to feel welcomed at your church?
- What things can you do to help a former prisoner make the shift from prison culture to civilian culture?
- How long do you think it will take for a person to make the shift from prison culture to civilian culture?

# The Process of Re-enculturation

## In the Last Session:

- The hopes and fears of church members and prisoners
- The elements of prison culture and criminogenic factors
- The difference between jails and prisons

## Objectives of This Session:

- Understand the time and effort it will take to help a former prisoner adapt.
- Recognize the differences between a systemic approach and a programmatic approach.
- Appreciate the seven keys that will make the process successful.

## Content

**I. The Goal of Onesimus Is to Help the Prisoner Change from Prison Culture to Outside Culture.**

A. It takes time and it takes a community.

B. Twelve months of continued influence is required for lasting change from prison culture and criminal thinking.[1]

**II. Program vs. Systemic Approach**

A. Program approach from the social service world

B. Systemic thinking[2]

---

1   Prison Fellowship Online Training, *Prison Culture, Module 3: Recognizing Criminal Thinking*, 2012.
2   *The Cat and the Toaster: Living System Ministry in a Technological Age*, Douglas A. Hall, 2010.

| Category | Program Thinking | Systems Thinking |
|---|---|---|
| Step One | Identify a need | Get inside the system and get to know the people. Be a learner. Fall in love with the people inside the system. |
| Step Two | Make a plan to address the need | Develop a mutual understanding |
| Step Three | Work the plan but create unintended consequences | Meet their stated short-term needs, but also meet their long-term, underlying needs |
| Step Four | Observe results: when the problem isn't solved (or gets worse) give up or double our efforts | Empower them to take over from you and reproduce |
| Essential Tools | Money, technology, organization | Relationship, inter-relationship, empowerment |

A. Examples of program thinking

    1. Eliminating poverty in America

    2. Eliminating global hunger

B. Examples of systems thinking

    1. The ministry of Jesus

    2. World Impact's incarnational approach to ministry among the urban poor

## III. Application to the Onesimus Workshop

A. Program thinking

B. Systemic thinking

C. The bottom line: To achieve the vision of welcoming former prisoners into your church for building up the body of Christ, you must take a systemic, relational, kingdom approach, not a programmatic, social-service approach.

## IV. Systemic Ways to Help Former Prisoners Transition to Civilian Life

A. Criminogenic factors and TUMI (see Appendix 1)

1. Beliefs

a. Sense of entitlement

b. Unrealistic perceptions of reality

c. Blaming others

d. Confusing wants with needs

2. Connections with peers

3. Personality habits

4. Broken families

5. Impulsive behavior

B. Factors that do NOT correlate to recidivism[3]

1. Low self-esteem

2. Mental health

3. Low educational level

4. Lack of employment

---

3   https://www.prisonfellowship.org/resources/training-resources/in-prison/on-going-ministry/criminogenic-needs-risk-returning-prison/?utm_source=NEWS&utm_medium=EMAIL&utm_campaign=PF-AWR&utm_term=NEWS&utm_content=risks%20of%20recidivism&spMailingID=17753810&spUserID=MTI0MjkyMzYwNzk0S0&spJobID=1062106038&spReportId=MTA2MjEwNjAzOAS2

## V. Seven Keys to Success

A. You don't have to do it all.

B. The process has to start months before release.

1. Before release (see Appendix 2,3)

2. Upon release[4]

   a. First three hours

   b. First three days

   c. First three months

   d. First three quarters

3. After release

C. Believe in the person as an asset rather than a liability.

1. Ignorance

2. Pity

3. Patronizing

4. Partnership

D. Patient, understanding friends who empower by setting boundaries

1. More than a job, housing, or money, they need a circle of friends.

2. Coach them to make decisions on their own.

3. Help them when they feel overwhelmed.

4. Be aware of manipulation.

---

4   https://www.prisonfellowship.org/resources/support-friends-family-of-prisoners/supporting-successful-prisoner-reentry/get-out-stay-out-reentry-guide/

5. When you help, honor them.

6. Be available.

7. Have a whole-church community of helpers.

E. Provide appropriate service opportunities in the church.

1. Avoid two mistakes:

    a. The person will *never be useful.*

    b. The person can be *immediately useful.*

2. Don't treat the person as a celebrity.

3. Provide a road map for the faithful (see Appendix 4).

F. Maintain high standards.

1. Challenge them to meet civilian expectations.

2. Be patient and forgiving as they adjust and grow

3. Push them beyond their comfort zone

4. Invest in the faithful.

G. Be aware of the cultural dynamics.

1. The former prisoner is struggling to shift from prison culture to civilian culture

2. There is a second potential cultural shift as well.

## Culture and Return

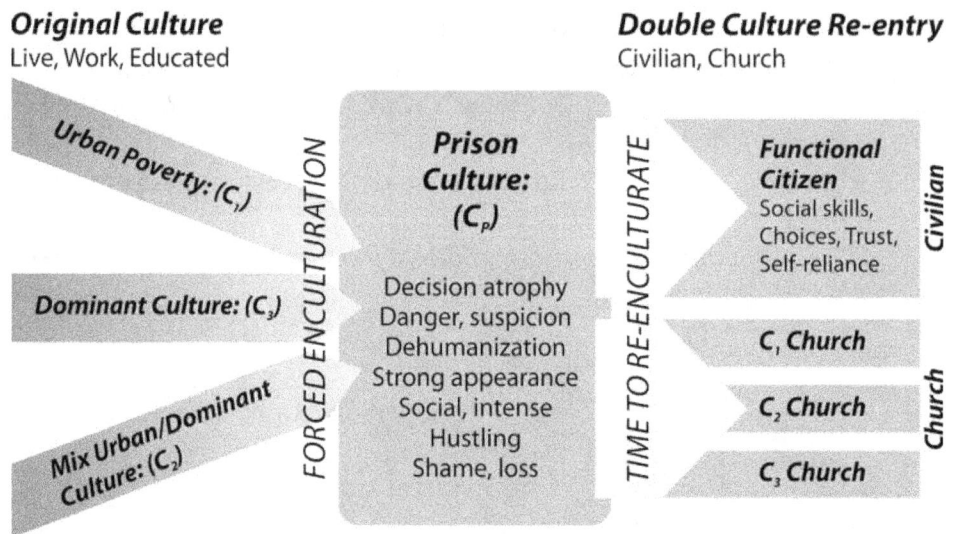

**Original Culture**
Live, Work, Educated

**Double Culture Re-entry**
Civilian, Church

Urban Poverty: $(C_1)$

Dominant Culture: $(C_3)$

Mix Urban/Dominant Culture: $(C_2)$

FORCED ENCULTURATION

**Prison Culture: $(C_p)$**

Decision atrophy
Danger, suspicion
Dehumanization
Strong appearance
Social, intense
Hustling
Shame, loss

TIME TO RE-ENCULTURATE

**Functional Citizen**
Social skills,
Choices, Trust,
Self-reliance

Civilian

$C_1$ Church

$C_2$ Church

$C_3$ Church

Church

**VI. Case Studies (see Appendix 5-6)**

**Summary of This Session**

- The best way to help a former prisoner adapt to civilian culture is through relationships, not a program.

- There are seven keys to success: prisoner motivation, cultural fit, starting early, need for friends, partnership mentality, providing for appropriate service opportunities, holding to high standards.

- Keep the end in mind. The end goal is empowerment: eventually handing over ministry to them – not simply keeping them out of prison.

**In the Next and Final Session, We Will Seek To:**

- Understand the tools World Impact offers.

- Outline the three essential next steps.

- Explain eight options for implementation.

**Questions for Discussion**

- Does a whole-church, relational approach make you feel liberated or do you prefer taking a programmatic approach to helping former prisoners?

- Which of the criminogenic factors seems most significant to you?

- When you consider the Seven Keys to Success, do you feel like they are achievable or overwhelming? Why?

# *The Next Steps*

## In the Last Session We Attempted To:

- Understand the difference between a programmatic approach and a systems, relational approach.

- Identify the criminogenic factors that contribute to recidivism.

- Define the seven keys to success that will help former prisoners transition from prison culture to civilian culture.

## Objectives of This Session:

- Understand the tools World Impact offers.

- Outline the three essential next steps.

- Explain eight options for implementation.

- Decide which initial steps you will take.

## Content

## I. The Tools World Impact Offers

*For information on these resources and more, visit* **www.tumi.org/about**.

   A. *Fight the Good Fight of Faith* (see Appendix 1 and 12)

   B. The SIAFU Network (see Appendix 13)

   C. TUMI Satellite (see Appendix 7 and 14)

   D. Internship program (see Appendix 4)

   E. The Evangel Network and Evangel School of Urban Church Planting (see Appendix 15)

   F. Church Associations (see Appendix 16)

   G. Prayer Resources: Let God Arise! Prayer Network (see Appendix 17)

## II. Three Essential Steps

A. Create a service path for the whole church.

B. Determine your initial level participation.

C. Orient the entire congregation.

## III. Create a Service Path for the Whole Church

A. How to make disciples for all members

B. Empower spiritual formation and leadership development for all members.

C. Release all members to ministry.

### Develop a Path for the Church (All Members)

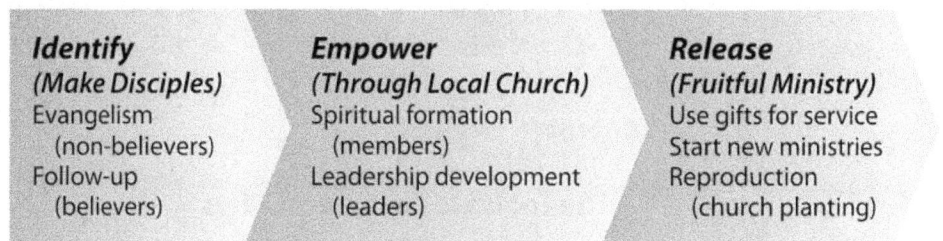

| Identify (Make Disciples) | Empower (Through Local Church) | Release (Fruitful Ministry) |
|---|---|---|
| Evangelism (non-believers) | Spiritual formation (members) | Use gifts for service Start new ministries |
| Follow-up (believers) | Leadership development (leaders) | Reproduction (church planting) |

Key: Create a system for strategic growth

D. Example

### World Impact Resources for Church Service Path

```
  Evangelism                              Enhanced Church Service
  Non-believers                                    Leaders
   e.g. Alpha

        │
        ▼                                       Church Planting
    Follow-up                                    New Churches
     Believers                              TUMI Evangel Resources
Fight the Good Fight of Faith
        │              │
        │              ▼
        │        Leader Development
        │              Leaders
        │      TUMI Satellite: Capstone Curriculum
        │
        ▼                            New Church Ministries
 Spiritual Formation                       Members
      Members
    SIAFU Groups
                                     Enhanced Church Service
                                            Members
```

## IV. Determine Your Initial Level Participation

A. Eight options

1. Organized prayer

2. Become more educated

3. Get to know prisoners before they are released

   *This can be done by contacting prison and jail ministries in your area, connecting with the families of prisoners through programs like Angel Tree (a program of Prison Fellowship), or contacting local representatives of national ministries like Kairos and Prison Fellowship.*

4. Start a TUMI satellite

5. Start a SIAFU chapter

6. Offer an internship

7. Connect with local resources (see Appendix 8)

8. Plant a church designed to welcome former prisoners

B. As the Spirit leads, choose among the eight options initially, and possibly pursue others at a later time

## V. Orient the Entire Congregation

A. Repeat from the pulpit that welcoming former prisoners is part of the vision of this church.

B. Involve people based on their gifting, or area of interest.

C. Give the former prisoner several names of people they can phone or text at any time, day or night.

D. Do things together.

E. Remember that prisoners have families and friends who need to be welcomed to the church.

## VI. Summary

A. The background and vision of the Onesimus Workshop

B. An understanding of what prison culture is like

C. How to help former prisoners make the transition from prison to civilian life

D. Provide tools and options for taking the next steps

**VII. A Final Word**

**Questions for Discussion**

- What has been the most exciting or interesting part of this workshop?
- What do you think God is saying to us as a result of this workshop?
- What do you think should be the next steps for our church?

# Appendix

Appendix 1
# TUMI Curriculum and Criminogenic Factors

TUMI's *Capstone Curriculum* (seminary training) and *Fight the Good Fight of Faith* (introduction to Christian faith), both address the factors that contribute to recidivism:

**Beliefs:** Thinking errors that affect how prisoners interpret and process information such as entitlement, self-justification, blaming others, unrealistic perceptions of reality, taking on a "victim stance" (for example, "the system is out to get me"), misinterpretation of harmless remarks as threats ("he disrespected me"), confusing wants with needs.

> *TUMI Curriculum: Helping prisoners to think biblically through study, discussion, reading, writing, memorizing. They receive new information to help them start thinking differently. This results in genuine sorrow for their crimes and a desire for restitution.*

**Peers:** Associating primarily with friends involved in criminal behavior puts one at high risk of sharing in that behavior. Over time, the incarcerated person loses contact with "prosocial" people, and then has no social support network to help reinforce appropriate behaviors. Choice of companions may actually be the greatest predictor of criminal behavior.

> *TUMI Curriculum: Forming cohort learning groups where prisoners learn and process together in Christian community.*

**Personality:** Habits of deceit, irresponsibility, aggression, violence, or impulsiveness; failure to conform to social norms and laws; reckless disregard for others' safety; little remorse for their mistreatment of others; substance abuse.

> *TUMI Curriculum: Students observe each other's behaviors 24/7 and hold them to account. TUMI students are leaders and must to demonstrate a higher standard of behavior. Also, the modeling of volunteers' Christian lives is a powerful influence for prisoners. This results in a new respect for authority and desire to conform with rules of civilian behavior.*

**Family dysfunction:** Broken families, abusive or neglectful relationships, permissiveness, family members involved in drug or alcohol abuse or criminal activities.

> *TUMI Curriculum: Students process their past through discussion of dozens of case studies that directly relate to their experience.*

**Low self-control:** A history of impulsive, risk-taking behavior; easily persuaded by situational factors. They often lack healthy attachments to positive friends, family, or employment, so there is little to constrain them from risky or criminal behavior.

> *TUMI Curriculum: The discipline needed to complete the programs breaks habits of laziness, victimhood, and impulsive behavior. This leads to self-control and a desire to be a servant leader who wants to help others.*

Through TUMI's curriculum, prisoners engage in active learning where they have to think for themselves, make decisions, and draw conclusions that result in lasting transformation.

APPENDIX 2
## *Guidelines for Prisoner Correspondence*
Adapted from Prison Fellowship's "Visit Prison in an Envelope"

### Consider Your Audience: Issues Prisoners Are Thinking About

1.  Facing uncertainty: Most prisoners, especially if they have been incarcerated for more than one year, are scared of reentry into society. They are hopeful, frightened, paranoid about doing everything right, and apprehensive about what they will face. Their movements have been absolutely controlled for years. They have not driven vehicles, not made choices, not had to exercise any discipline about when to get up, when to eat or how to spend money. Former prisoners often tell of the panic they feel when confronted with a menu at a restaurant or the bewildering array of choices on the supermarket shelf. Technology has moved on while they were incarcerated. They may not know how to use an ATM machine or a gas pump where you pay by credit card. Very few have had access to computers so word processing, spreadsheets, the Internet, E-mail, web pages and related computer skills can be foreign and so they panic when they think of how necessary those skills are to compete in the job market. They also know they have a multiyear gap on their resume to explain.

2.  Family dynamics: When one partner goes to prison, an estimated 85% of marriages fail. Many prisoners have broken family relationships they must now face in person upon release.

3.  The importance of friends: A church contact can help prepare the way for a receptive welcome upon release. One returning citizen said, "Every prisoner who gets out that doesn't have a Christian program to lean on will go back to the same town, the same friends – or so-called friends – and will get into the same old stuff. They need Christian support on the outside."

### Beware of the Common Pitfalls:
### Even TUMI Students May Have Mixed Motives

1.  Scams: some may try to take advantage of your kindness for financial gain.

2.  Romantic attachments: some are interested in building a relationship that leads to romance.

3.  Legal help: some may ask for assistance for leniency, pardon or post-conviction help.

4.  Prison advocacy: some may complain of unfair treatment and abuse by prison system or staff and ask for help in changing the institution.

**Dos and Don'ts**

1.  Always

    a.  Offer encouragement and inspiration (prisoners are well aware of their failures).

    b.  Speak God's Word, but don't preach or patronize – these students are TUMI students.

    c.  Use a P.O. Box or an office address as the return address (rather than your home address).

2.  Never

    a.  Contact anyone on behalf of a prisoner.

    b.  Send a gift or items requested by a prisoner.

    c.  Give legal advice or counsel regarding a prisoner's case or write a letter to the parole board on behalf of the prisoner.

    d.  Send money for financial support or legal fees. Don't co-sign loans or process money orders.

    e.  Ask why a prisoner is incarcerated.

    f.  Give out your telephone number or agree to receive collect calls.

    g.  Provide personal information or share personal problems with a prisoner.

    h.  Send unused stamps to a prisoner – this is currency on the inside.

APPENDIX 3
## *Forming a Plan Before Release*

This list can be used to help former prisoners develop a plan prior to their release, so they can begin implementation immediately. Because their decision-making skills have atrophied, they will likely need help to be proactive before they leave prison. Many prisoners will wait until they get released to start reacting to circumstances, having no advanced plan in place. Since they have lost their time-management skills, they are vulnerable to being overwhelmed by all the changes they experience upon release. Here are some questions you can ask to help prisoners form a plan before they are released.

1. Where will you live? If you assume that friends or family are housing you, have you clearly communicated that expectation?

2. Who will pick you up at the gate?

3. What will your schedule be on the first day you are released?

4. What parenting responsibilities will you have? What expectations do others have for you regarding parenting?

5. What household responsibilities will you have (chores, paying bills, transportation)? What do others expect from you in these areas?

6. What plans do you have for employment or education? If there is not a job or schooling waiting, what are your job-search plans?

7. What family or friends do you want to visit when you get out and how many hours per week are planned for these visits? How will you avoid wasting too much time getting re-connected when you need to spend time on other tasks?

8. What physical needs do you have such as a driver's license, birth certificate, Social Security card? What can be secured before release vs. what needs to be pursued after release?

9. What expectations do you have for finances, and what do others expect of you financially? Do you have a checking account?

10. Where will you attend church, or which churches will you visit upon release? How do you plan to get connected with a small group or mentor?

11. What friends and family should you avoid in order to associate with only positive influences?

12. If you have substance abuse in your past, how will you be proactive to keep dealing with that, avoiding the naive notion that you are immune from temptation?

13. If you have children, how have they changed since incarceration and what are they thinking about your release?

14. What elements of prison culture do you see in yourself that need to be open to correction as you shift to civilian culture?

15. What do you need to purchase, e.g. clothes, toiletries?

16. What needs to be done about filing taxes?

17. What needs to be done about child support obligations or parole requirements?

18. How will you safeguard yourself against wasting time on new technologies such as video games, online shopping, gambling, or pornography?

# Church Internships
Rev. Dr. Don L. Davis

Perhaps the most effective method of training leaders to serve in the church is practical internships. This is not unique to church life; dozens of guilds and industries employ internships and apprenticeships as the chosen way of producing their new generation of workers and leaders. Combining the rigors of hard intellectual study, practical experience, and supervised feedback, internships are a powerful and effective way to multiply leaders capable of producing tangible results in diverse study programs. In the same way as is used in such fields as medicine, law, and industry, we can powerfully equip qualified emerging leaders who once were incarcerated to become godly, effective servants of Christ serving in a particular role in the local church. By emphasizing good selection, careful and capable supervision, meaningful assignments, and regular feedback, we can help budding Christian workers to gain invaluable training in a variety of positions, tasks, and roles needed in the life of the church.

## Definition of Ministry Internships
Ministry internships are pre-defined terms of service and learning sponsored in the context of a supportive church/ministry, overseen by capable supervision which is designed to equip the intern in some specific task of church ministry and mission. Look at these elements:

- "Pre-defined terms of service and learning." Church internships should be limited to a specific term of service, with specific rules and guidelines for its length and work. We strongly suggest that some kind of specific, written contract of service be created, spelling out precisely the bounds, privileges, and responsibilities of the internship, including its length, any remuneration offered, terms of service, and all other matters related to the intern's work and duties.

- ". . . in the context of a supportive church/ministry." Church internships should be connected to a particular church or ministry which has formally agreed to oversee the intern, providing specific training and exposure to an important element of its outreach and service.

- ". . . overseen by capable supervision." Church internships should be connected to specific mentors, supervisors, or leaders who supervise and oversee the intern's assignment and work.

Interns should report to these supervisors who provide information on the character of the assignment, and give regular feedback as to the intern's progress or areas of growth needed to be worked on.

- ". . . which is designed to equip the intern in some specific task of church ministry and mission." Church internships for emerging leaders should be targeted to equip the worker in a specific task that furthers the mission and purpose of the church or one of its ministries. Internships should not be "special" in the sense of creating some unique and unrelated role for the intern. Rather, the best church internships are connected specifically to training a worker to gain expertise and exposure to a task or assignment that the church currently embraces and supports, or is being created to enhance the church's goals and priorities.

A practical, well-defined, and carefully supervised internship for workers who have proven their worth is a great tool to equip believers who are former prisoners to gain the necessary knowledge, mentoring, and exposure to real life ministry experience. As a church intern we cannot merely provide that growing disciple with excellent training, we must also equip a worker who can, under the Spirit's direction, become a valuable member of a healthy church's effective team of ministers.

**Designing Leadership Development That Succeeds**

As in the case of all intern candidates, it will be critical that each applicant be carefully screened and vetted in order to ensure both their readiness to participate in your program, with the blessing and confirmation of your leaders. Great care and focus must be decided well in advance of the learning experience to guarantee its success. In other words, your ministry supervisors must take the time to map out a measurable and feasible ministry training plan, an overall intern schedule, and the kinds of learning projects the internship will include. In addition, time must be given to determine the substance of the internship, including ministry assignments, time for study and critical reflection, and whatever financial resources and staff support the internship will provide. *Until these critical features have been carefully considered and decided, no internship program should be commenced!*

Jesus taught his disciples as ministry interns, selecting them to be with him and to send them out to preach (cf. Mark 3.14). Through association with the Master, observing his work and engaging him regarding the meaning and significance of his ministry, the disciples became the leaders of the Church. Through their interaction with Christ in the context of real life, they became effective ministers of the gospel, and were able to train others to train others.

**First Things First:**
**Basic Convictions of Church Internships for Former Prisoners**

In order for a ministry internship program to work, we as oversight providers must lay a proper foundation. An internship is not just a job opportunity. It is a ministry which is built upon a solid biblical theology. All of the internship's programs, activities, and functions build on the biblical framework for ministry. The clearer you are about your assumptions at the beginning of the program, the more likely it will be that your program will be effective.

*Allow for time to adjust to civilian life:*
*Let former prisoners learn to be members of the church.*

One of the first mistakes you can make in discipling former prisoners is to rush God's leading and preparation in their lives. During the first year they should be careful to focus on finding a church and small group, offering their gifts in service, finding a job, mending relationships, and adjusting their attitudes and actions to conform with life on the outside.

*Do not quickly lay hands on potential candidates:*
*Give former prisoners time to prove their discipleship in the body.*

Be wary to encourage a budding Christian disciple recently released from prison to engage in significant ministry leadership such as pastoring, church planting, leading Bible studies or small groups. They should concentrate on being a solid member of the body, participating in its church life, using their gifts in the church under pastoral leadership and in connection with the church's duly authorized leaders during this year of transition.

*Recognize and take into account the*
*unspoken assumptions of the congregation.*

Do not be offended at your congregation's concerns about incorporating former prisoners into its church family. A significant part of a congregation's maturity in Christ is its ability to welcome and receive into its family new members who require a special reception and acceptance. "May the God of endurance and encouragement grant you to live in such harmony with one another, in accord with Christ Jesus, that together you may with one voice glorify the God and Father of our Lord Jesus Christ. Therefore welcome one another as Christ has welcomed you, for the glory of God" Rom. 15.5-7 (ESV). It may take time for a congregation to learn how to live in grace and love, and to overcome its natural inclinations to misjudge or stereotype believers in your midst who were formerly incarcerated. Because the congregation may feel unsafe to have former prisoners in the service, some churches have recruited ex-offenders as security staff to provide a sense of safety. This is an effective way to help former prisoners take a first step toward more significant places of service over time.

### Take adequate time to plan out specifically the elements of the church internships you will offer.

In order to ensure your program is successful, you will need to think through carefully the various elements of the church internship you intend to offer. While the particular assignments will vary greatly depending on your congregational needs and opportunities, most effective internships will include at least three critical components. First, the skills of life, both as a responsible disciple in society and as a member of the church. Second, biblical and theological training related to the role of servant leadership in the church, and specifically in the role that the intern will play in your congregation. Finally, a careful outline of the specific ministry responsibilities they will assume during their internship, and how those responsibilities will be carried out over the term of the internship. For a thorough and more helpful discussion of mapping out your particular church internship program please go to *www.tumi.org/onesimus* for details.

### Always think with two brains: One which concentrates on the particular role of the internship and the other that recognizes the candidate's future calling and gifting in ministry.

While a successful internship is to be greatly desired, we must always remember that God may have even greater ends for the interns he provides us. Although it may not be God's will for every former prisoner to become a pastor, church planter, or Christian worker, there is no question that the Holy Spirit will call some of them to these noble tasks in ministry. We are believing God to raise up an army of qualified spiritual laborers among the formerly incarcerated to plant, pastor, and build up healthy new churches that will be both welcoming and culturally conducive to former prisoners! World Impact has specifically set up systems and processes within its Evangel School of Urban Church Planting to help discern and equip former prisoners with these callings and gifts to navigate their way into those ministries. If you discover in any intern candidate the gift and calling to do ongoing pastoral, church planting, and ministry or missions outreach, do not hesitate to connect them to us at *www.tumi.org/evangel* to receive help, encouragement, and advice in how to help them enter the process of discernment regarding those opportunities.

**Conclusion: The Necessity of Church-based Internships**

Of all the tools provided to the church to raise up new leaders, nothing compares to healthy, well-supervised church internships. Whatever the scope, however the form, a practical, life-based, and church-connected internship can help emerging Christian leaders discover their calling and gifting in ministry, and offer invaluable help to the congregation to grow. We must do all we can to help identify, equip, and release former prisoners who have named the name of Christ to discover their unique call to ministry, in order that they may play their part in advancing the Kingdom, under the Spirit's direction and the church's oversight.

Appendix 5

# Case Study:
# What Happened When I Got Out (Dan's Story)
*Spiritual Survival Guide: For Prison and Beyond*, p. 175.

About six months ago, before I went home it occurred to me that I was really going home. I became very anxious. Everything started bothering me. Inmates were driving me nuts. I found new hatred for the guards. Standing in chow lines made my heart pound. And if I couldn't get on the phone when I wanted to, I about lost my mind. The funny thing was that I knew all of these attitudes were my problem. I knew nothing had changed with my surroundings; something must have changed in me. I knew I had short timer's disease.

I took some action. I prayed about it – going so far as to pray for the inmates and guards I was getting angry at. I talked about it in my recovery meetings and with fellow believers. These things helped but didn't seem to take it away. About five minutes after I woke up each day my brain would start with anxiety and resentment.

It was so surprising to me to feel so stressed about going home. I felt more stressed about leaving than I did about coming to prison.

For a long time, it had been easier for me to focus on daily prison life. I really didn't want to think about the family, women, and friends that I'd left behind. That was too painful for me. To me, leaving prison was going to be the end of all my problems. I pictured a warm welcome from family, old friends, past girlfriends. I figured that some would give me a job. In prison, I did a lot of working out so my physical health was good. Most importantly, in prison I'd prayed, read the Bible, and was involved in a 12-Step program. I really believed that going home would be like going to Disneyland. No more crazy inmates, guards, staff. No more "celly problems." No more waiting for money in the mail or commissary. I was going to actually be free! In my deepest heart, I believed that my transition would be filled with stress-free laughter and goodwill from the world. Nothing could have been further from the truth.

Prayer definitely helped during this time. So did talking with fellow believers-people I could trust. They advised that I continue to pray, read the Bible and find others to help, even if helping meant nothing more than a short, kind word or deed.

On the way home I got car sick. I hadn't been in a car for years and motion made me ill. As soon as I arrived at my parents' house I was filled with a sense of guilt and shame. I didn't know what exactly to do next. All of the bright color of everyday life in the real world sort of scared me. Right away I felt like I didn't fit.

Some good friends came by – friends who are sober and walking in a spiritual path. I knew they'd understand just what I was going through. They didn't. How could they – they'd never been to prison for years like I just had. They were a bit confused as to why I seemed uptight. I tried to explain but was not sure myself. I mean, "Wow, I'm actually home. So why do I feel so weird and afraid?"

I was honest with everyone. I told my friends and family that being home was like being in some alien landscape. That I didn't know what to do with my hands. After a few days I began to notice people sort of losing interest in the novelty of Dan being home. I wanted to call everyone and say, "Hey, don't lose interest, I'm home now and want to be part of life!" People just got on with their lives, and I felt alone and afraid. I literally didn't know what should I be doing every day.

I had a basic understanding that I needed to continue my sobriety through spiritual channels. To me that meant daily prayer, Bible reading, AA, and basic "golden rule" living. I did some of that, but to be honest I did more worrying about what people thought about me and where I was going to find a job. My relationship with God quickly went on the back burner.

I kept saying to myself, "Look what you have done with your life! How will you ever repair it? How will you ever get a job? And what's up with my girl? She seems to be acting weird." It was like at every turn, I felt more and more out of place. Even those old friends seemed unsure about what to say to me. I felt like the world had a secret it wouldn't let me in on. I began to unravel.

We all want to feel connected with God and people. There's nothing worse than feeling alone. After a few weeks home I felt more alone than when I was in prison. My friends in recovery were busy with family, work, and school. At church I felt little in common with these God people. I know the pastor says they don't judge, but who doesn't judge? Are there people who really don't judge? So down I went.

In hindsight I missed the turn when I began to care more about what people thought about me than what I was actually doing in my life. My focus became about what I thought others were thinking about me – rather than just doing my very best to do the next right thing. My mind ran round and round, and I forgot the lessons that had been beaten into me by life, in prison, and my search for God. I was back to relying on my own broken thinking.

After a serious relapse I knew I had to find a way to really stay on track. Lots of us go off the path many times. The real deal is to stay on it when the going gets tough and uncertain. I moved into a halfway house. I began to see that my troubles are about me and not about how the world treated me. I saw that I needed to put real effort into getting positive results if I wanted any. For most of my life I'd found ways of manipulating people to build the life that I wanted. I was always more interested in looking good than doing good. I saw that attitude had to stop.

*What happened to Dan is a great example of the complicated challenges of reentry, and how tough it can be for many of us trying to survive spiritually on the outside. It isn't just Dan's story; nearly all of us have a story dealing with our own case of "short-timer's disease," unrealistic expectations, a lack of careful planning and communication, the awkward experience to adapting to life on the outside, and the sobering realization that life is wonderful, but hard.*

APPENDIX 6
## *TUMI Prisoner Advice for Reentry*

### Greg's Story

First, please stay prayerful and remain hopeful. God's got you. While nothing was as I was told, I am blessed! So amazingly, wonderfully blessed! For starters, initially I had no housing. I was homeless but got into a "sober-living" bed through B.I. (Behavioral Interventions), a division of GEO Corp. I also signed up with Veterans Community Services for housing assistance, but B.I. got me housed first. The Lord has shown me much favor, including showing me the spot where I slept when I was homeless.

I got EBT asap, which typically is $194 every month. Once I got the EBT card and an I.D. card I was able to get an "Obama phone," with unlimited talk and text plus 500 MB data. As a homeless EBT recipient I was able to go to several fast food restaurants to eat hot meals.

I only go to the office for monthly UA's. Employment was sporadic, but I got hired here at the Plaza Hotel one year ago, and I am full-time, working the front desk two days per week and three days maintenance. God is good, all the time!

Additionally, I see God bringing healing in my family relationships, including my wife. I know He is working behind the scenes, and occasionally gives me glimpses to bolster my faith.

Now as to the where I am with regard to the local Body of Christ. God has me on a mission. He has opened the doors for me to share His testimony of what He did in my life to encourage others and lay the foundation for continued support and future ministry. God connected me to a TUMI brother in ministry and I have opportunities to share at those services. I wrapped up my ninth module in TUMI, and I hope to complete the program. I have received manifold blessings. I am blessed by the best! Woo-Hoo!

All in all, I've had some challenges, and with that some periods of depression and extreme sadness. Yet, at the end of the day, God is faithful. He always comes through, though not on my schedule. His grace is my provision. Without it I would not be doing as well as I am.

Stay prayerful, stay hopeful, and stay connected to the body. For "In him we live and move and have our being' as even some of your own poets have said, 'For we are indeed his offspring'" Acts 17.28 (ESV). "For this reason I also suffer these things; nevertheless I am not ashamed, for I know whom I have believed and am persuaded that He is able to keep what I have committed to Him until that Day." 2 Tim. 1.12-13 (NKJV).

## Martin's Story

I am writing to tell you a little about my re-integration into society after 22 years in California State Prison. I was scheduled to go to a home upon release, but a week before my parole I was told I would be going to another place. To tell the truth I was very disappointed at this change which was out of my control. Next, I was told that I would not be picked up by the agency and would have to take the train and bus (it was actually two trains and two buses). Furthermore, when I asked my counselor to call and ask how I would make it to the program from the train station, I was told to just get a taxi or something. I was now devastated and disappointed.

This background information is written to explain what I've found to be most important about coming back to society after being in prison for so long, and it's building relationships and networking. I was blessed when I arrived at the train station (8 pm on Sunday night) to have two ex-lifers, who I served with in ministry within prison, pick me up. These men helped me to navigate all of the many different roads I would have to travel in order to get "established" as a returning citizen.

Some things that are necessary and important:

1. You are going to need ID. If you don't have your birth certificate (have your family) order it. If you had a driver's license that's less than 25 years old you may still be in the system.

2. You're going to need a Social Security Card (you need a California ID or DL for this).

3. Patience! All the programs are different. Whether they grant day passes, let you use their phones, take you to appointments is of little consequence. Eventually, you will be granted access and opportunities to move around, explore, and it will be up to you to make good and wise decisions.

Seek out a group of knowledgeable people to help you! Seek out the lifers groups, ministries, and parole resources set in place to help you.

Be open and honest with your parole agent! Call him often and ask a lot of questions! Be persistent and don't take "no" for an answer! Use the library and career center to help you. Learn to use computers and the internet.

Above all, get hooked up with God's people. Find a good church home. I hope this was helpful. Be thankful to God for your freedom. Do God's will and let him guide you through his Holy Spirit day by day.

**Kevin's Story**
This is from an ex-lifer that just did twenty-seven years in California. I have been out six and one-half months. I do not have all the answers, so let me share with you what I do know.

I will tell you everything has changed. I will tell you that the worst day out here, is still better than the best day in there. Just as you worked for your parole date, you also have to work to be on parole. The best advice I can give to you is to keep a tally of all the money you spend because it doesn't last long.

If you were in prison for less than twenty-five years, you just pay a renewal fee for your driver's license as it is still active. If you were incarcerated for over twenty-five years you are no longer in the system. The first thing you have to do then is to acquire a birth certificate at the county hall of records. Then second thing you will need is a Social Security card. A DD-214 will work if you are a veteran. In acquiring your California I.D. you will need a birth certificate, and you will have to take the CDL written exam and the driver's test with a vehicle. Once you have done this you should receive your CDL + Social Security Card within a few weeks.

When you are released you will also qualify for Medical. Always remember to try to have a positive attitude.

We are more concerned about what people think of us or about us than they actually do.

Remember the Word of the Lord – it will always help you through if you are sincere about your new walk in life. There are an abundance of people that want to help; just ask. Be humble, honest, gracious and patient.

One day a couple weeks after you get out, it will hit you that you're truly free.

I will tell you if you have a brother or a sister in the Church to call, then do it. They will give words of encouragement, support and comfort.

The world out here is fleshly everywhere you turn. Everywhere you go there are sex and drugs. I can tell you if you don't stay grounded in faith, the desires of the worldly man will eat you.

I will say that surrounding yourself with like-minded brothers and sisters will help you stay grounded. Life is fast and expensive out here, it is doable. Find a solid base. Remember the Word of the Lord. It's not easy because there is no down time out here; you must set time for yourself.

Now you have completed the first part of the race by getting yourself paroled. The race is not over; it has just begun.

Appendix 7

# Tips on Transitioning Reentry Leaders into Outside TUMI Satellites

Rich Esselstrom

1. We try to make our TUMI classes consistent with what prisoners experienced on the inside. Students coming from prison will make comparisons between the two locations. At first, they will prefer the prison setting, having fond memories of their experience. They may even talk of how great their prison mentors were! Don't take it personally. You will grow on them! One comparison will be that we allow take home finals. This will surprise them. They will see this as being easy and maybe somewhat lax. Be prepared for this and remind them that it is closed book. This may or may not be an issue. It is just something to be aware of.

2. Be aware and maybe study prison culture. I have found some former inmates really like to talk and even be somewhat confrontational and dogmatic with certain issues. I think this stems from the fact that they need to know what they know on the inside and defend it. Don't let any one student dominate the conversation.

3. My experience has been that some former inmates who want to take classes won't be able to follow through for various reasons. They have a strong desire to get married. They are looking for and finding work. They move around. They don't have transportation. This is a big one. I would encourage the mentors not to provide transportation but to link them up with other students who they can carpool with or use public transportation. If they want to be there, they will make this happen.

4. These guys are a blessing, so welcome them into your class warmly. Hook them up with other students. TUMI can be a very valuable resource for them to help them thrive on the outside as Christian leaders. They will be very appreciative for the opportunity to continue their training and equipping with us. Don't treat them any differently and watch them grow!

5. Follow up on them quickly!!! Let them come and sit in on classes and feel a part of things until they can start a class from the beginning. These guys need Christians who are leaders and friends. Where better to find them than TUMI and the church?

APPENDIX 8
## *Finding Local Resources*

1.  The following is a list of possible local connections you can make to help people re-entering society from incarceration. Each community will have different services available, so you do not have to start up your own programs at your church. A great place for you to start is with the local rescue mission. Often they will already be aware of services offered in a particular city or surrounding area.

    a.  Churches and fellowship groups who welcome former prisoners

    b.  Employment

    c.  Transitional housing

    d.  Drug and alcohol programs

    e.  Legal services

    f.  Food and clothing

    g.  Transportation

    h.  Reentry organizations/ministries

    i.  Medical services

    j.  Parole and interaction with law enforcement

2.  As an example of a list of local services, see *www.underthedoor.org* for the Chicago area.

    Their annual directory: *www.underthedoor.org/red-chicago/current-edition* can be an example of something you can create in your community. Once you have done so, make the list available to others so they do not have to re-invent the wheel.

3.  Correctional Ministries and Chaplains Association (*www.cmcainternational.org*) is an association of various ministries involved in ministry to prisoners inside institutions and also reentry.

4.  Do a search for "Second Chance Month" activities in your community. This is a national effort to educate people about the realities returning citizens face, while celebrating their restoration and redemption.

5.  At *www.prisonfellowship.org*, do a search for "reentry" to find a wide variety of helpful ideas and resources.

6.  Helpful books

    a.  Fred Jay Nelson. *Spiritual Survival Guide for Prison and Beyond.*

    b.  Steve Corbett and Brian Fikkert. *When Helping Hurts: How to Alleviate Poverty without Hurting the Poor . . . and Yourself.*

Appendix 9
# *Resources for Essential Reentry Services*
Prison Fellowship

The goal of reentry ministry is to provide a continuum of care that helps ex-prisoners succeed in life on the outside. Needs in all areas of life must be addressed in order for returning citizens to be whole again.

Finding resources to help ex-prisoners is an ongoing activity for most reentry teams. Once the resources are identified, it is important to have a system for cataloging the information for easy retrieval in the future. Creating a computer database is one good way of organizing and managing these resources.

## National Organizations/Agencies
The following is a starter list of large nationally recognized organizations and agencies that offer a variety of services for ex-prisoners and their families. Most have very helpful websites explaining their services and providing information about their state and local offices. This is an excellent place to begin your research.

- *Catholic Charities USA:* Local Catholic Charities agencies help families and individuals who are homeless or in danger of becoming homeless or who struggle with racism and poverty. Being Catholic is not a requirement for receiving assistance.
  Phone: (703) 549-1390 *www.catholiccharitiesusa.org*

- *Goodwill Industries:* Goodwill Industries is one of the world's largest nonprofit providers of job training and employment services for people who have a history of welfare dependency, illiteracy, criminal history, and homelessness.
  Phone: (800) 466-9455 *www.goodwill.org*

- *Salvation Army:* The Salvation Army works in cooperation with prison, probation, and parole offices in prison rehabilitation and crime prevention. Services include job-training, employment opportunities, material aid, and spiritual guidance. Salvation Army rehabilitation centers and Harbor Light centers have been designated as halfway houses for ex-prisoners to participate in work-release programs.
  Phone: (703) 684-5500 *www.salvationarmyusa.org*

- *Social Security Administration (SSA):* The SSA can help ex-prisoners who need a replacement Social Security card or a Social Security number. Some ex-prisoners may be eligible for retirement benefits or disability assistance, depending on their age and health.

  Phone: (800) 772-1213 *www.ssa.gov*

- *U.S. Department of Labor Employment and Training Administration (ETA):* The ETA offers programs, resources, and online tools to help workers in all stages of job and career development, including job training programs and job placement services for economically disadvantaged adults. Locally, these programs are offered through workforce centers (also known as One-Stop centers or Job Service centers).

  Phone: (877) 872-5627 *www.doleta.gov*

- *United Way:* United Way's focus is on improving life for people in three areas: financial stability, education, and health. To promote financial stability, United Way supports programs that help families meet their basic needs, while also gaining the skills to obtain long-term financial goals such as manageable expenses, affordable housing, and adequate income to support their family.

  Phone: (703) 836-7112 or simply dial 211 *www.unitedway.org*

- *YMCA:* The Y offers services that help people be self-reliant, productive, and connected to the community. Local Ys address the unique needs of their communities and provide services focused on critical areas such as child welfare, community health, job training, environmental education, and family needs.

  Phone: (800) 872-9622 *www.ymca.net*

- *YWCA:* Local YWCAs provide services to meet the needs of women in their communities. Depending on local programs, these may include: child care, rape crisis intervention, domestic violence assistance, shelters for domestic violence victims and their families, job training, and career counseling.

  Phone: (202) 467-0801 *www.ywca.org*

## State-Level Resources

The following are a few important state agencies that are helpful with meeting the needs of ex-prisoners. Agency names may vary from state to state. The easiest way to find these resources is through your state's official website or the state government pages in most local phone books. This is not an exhaustive list, but a starting place for further research.

- *State Employment Commission:* Although the exact name may vary, all states have agencies that offer job training and rehabilitation, help people find employment, and promote the well-being of those in the workforce.

- *Housing Authority (Public Housing):* Housing Authority services vary, but usually include emergency shelters, housing for the homeless, housing for those with chronic substance abuse problems or mental illness, group homes, shelters, and transitional housing.

- *State and County Health Departments:* Medical and psychiatric services provided by state and county health departments vary, but this is a viable source of free or nearly free healthcare for ex-prisoners and their dependents.

- *Department of Health and Human Services:* Low-income households may qualify for the food stamp program offered by the state's Department of Health and Human Services. Each state has its own requirements and guidelines for receiving help.

- *Department of Motor Vehicles (DMV):* Most ex-prisoners will need to visit the local DMV office to obtain a new driver's license or for help with automobile registration and/or license tags. In some states, the DMV offers a picture ID card with an ID number for those who do not drive.

## Local Resources

Newly-released prisoners frequently need local community-support services. You can find available assistance in your community by searching the internet or contacting nearby churches, the public library, or the police department. The following are some examples of local resources that are very helpful with reentry ministries.

- *Food Banks:* To meet immediate needs for food, ex-prisoners may be referred to a local food bank or soup kitchen until they get food stamps and/or a job that provides regular income.

- *Temporary Shelters:* Many communities meet the short-term needs of the homeless by referring them to temporary shelters operated by government agencies, large non-profits, or private charities.

- *Public Health Clinics:* Help with prescription drugs, physical check-ups, and other medical needs may be available through low-cost health clinics operated by government agencies or private charities.

- *Resale Shops or Clothes Closets:* Help with clothing and basic household items is often found through local resale shops or clothes closets operated by churches or other non-profits.

- *Job Training Opportunities:* Most ex-prisoners don't have money to pay for job training, so they will need referrals to local businesses, government agencies, or non-profit groups that offer on-the-job training, apprenticeships, or other job-skill training.

Appendix 10

## Culture, Not Color: Interaction of Class, Culture, and Race

Rev. Dr. Don L. Davis

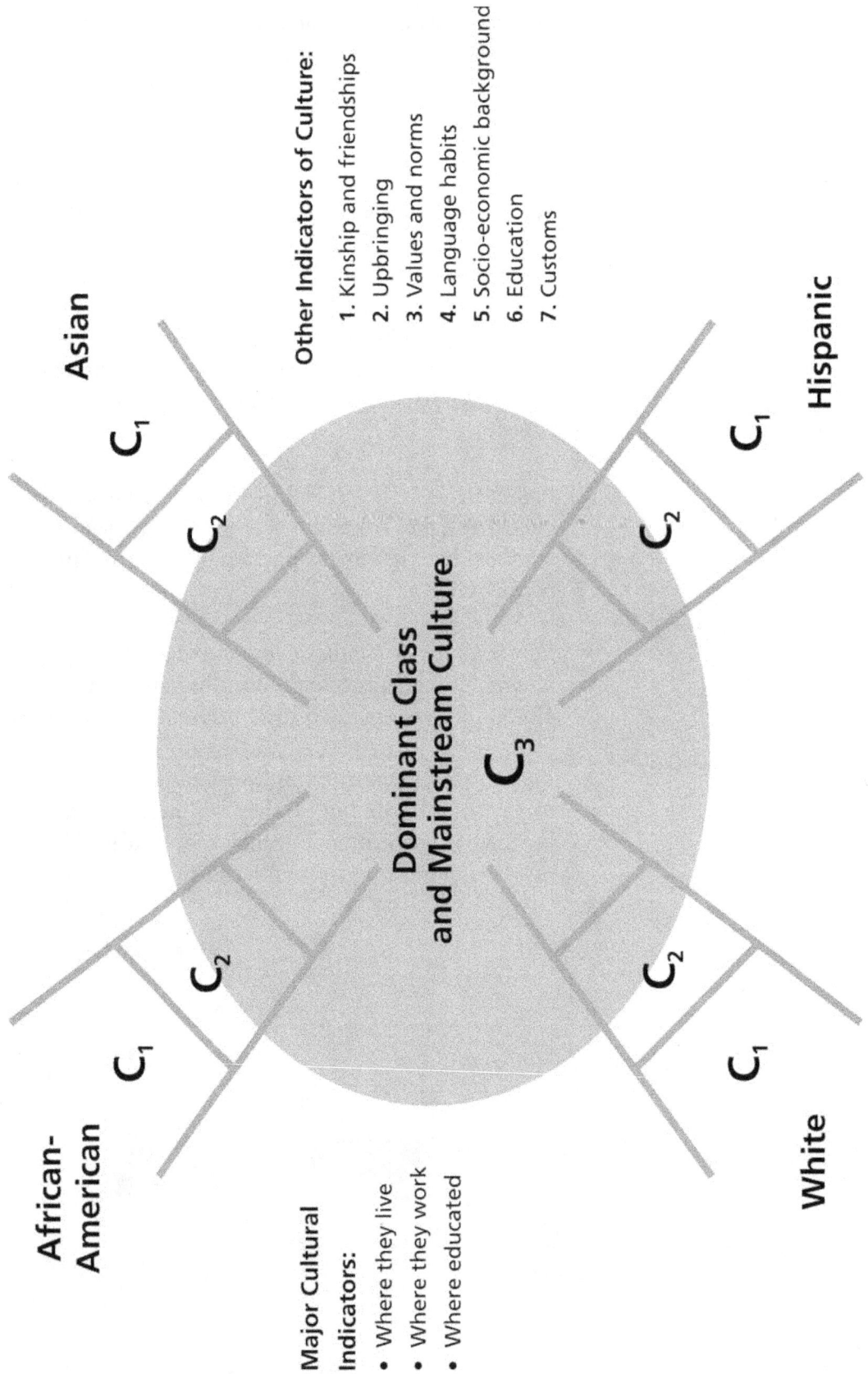

**Major Cultural Indicators:**

- Where they live
- Where they work
- Where educated

**Other Indicators of Culture:**

1. Kinship and friendships
2. Upbringing
3. Values and norms
4. Language habits
5. Socio-economic background
6. Education
7. Customs

Asian

$C_1$

$C_2$

Hispanic

$C_1$

$C_2$

**Dominant Class and Mainstream Culture**

$C_3$

African-American

$C_2$

$C_1$

$C_2$

$C_1$

White

APPENDIX 11

## Authentic Freedom in Jesus Christ

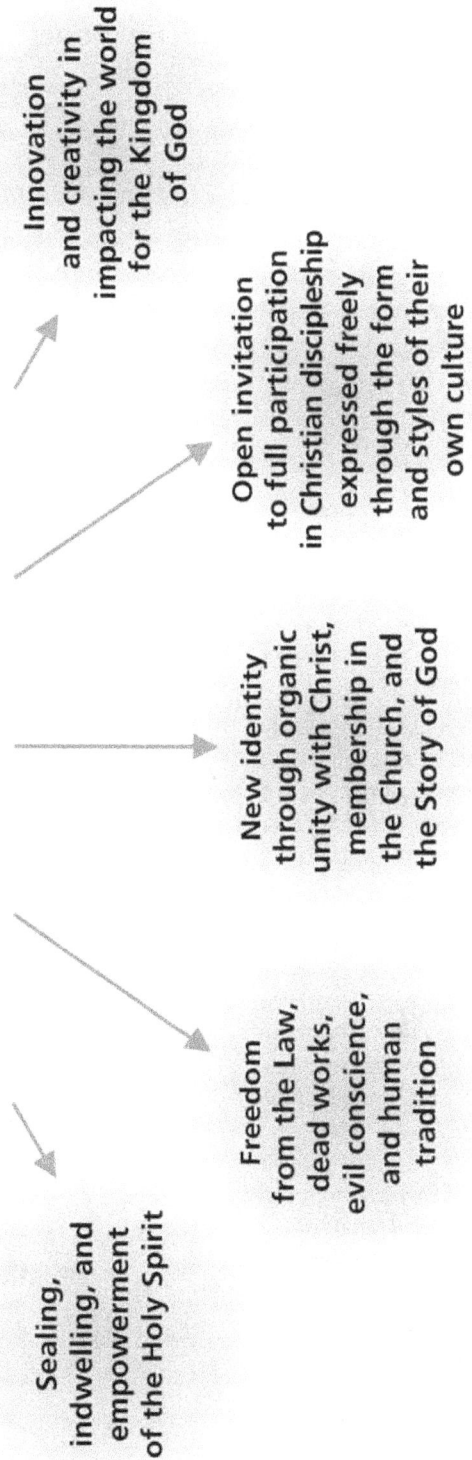

Rev. Dr. Don L. Davis

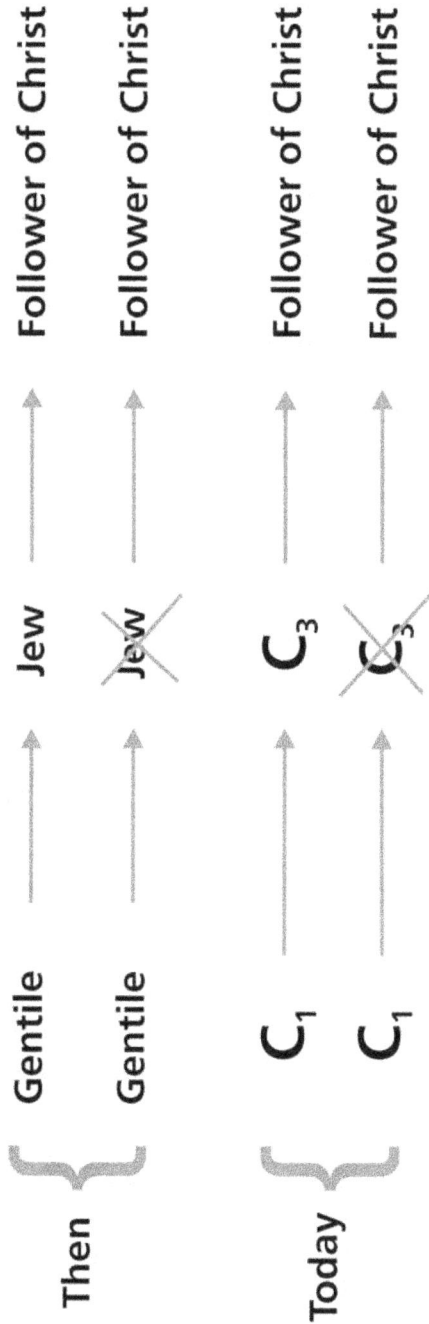

| | | |
|---|---|---|
| Then | Gentile → | Follower of Christ |
| | Jew → | Follower of Christ |
| | ~~Gentile~~ → | Follower of Christ |
| | ~~Jew~~ → | Follower of Christ |
| Today | $C_1$ → | Follower of Christ |
| | ~~$C_1$~~ → | Follower of Christ |
| | $C_3$ | |
| | ~~$C_3$~~ | |

## Authentic Freedom in Jesus Christ!

Sealing, indwelling, and empowerment of the Holy Spirit

Freedom from the Law, dead works, evil conscience, and human tradition

New identity through organic unity with Christ, membership in the Church, and the Story of God

Open invitation to full participation in Christian discipleship expressed freely through the form and styles of their own culture

Innovation and creativity in impacting the world for the Kingdom of God

APPENDIX 12

# *Fight the Good Fight of Faith: Playing Your Part in God's Unfolding Drama*
## *Sacred Roots[1] Follow-up Curriculum*

The Urban Ministry Institute

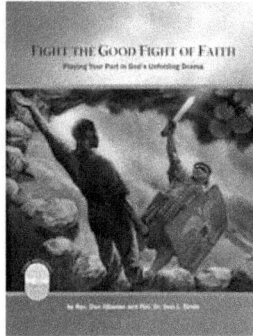

*Fight the Good Fight of Faith is adaptable for different audiences, ages, and venues.*

*Multiple translations are available through www.tumistore.org and Amazon.com. Some translations are available for Kindle.*

*[1] Sacred Roots is the name TUMI uses to describe the core confessions, practices, and councils of the Christian faith between the years 100 and 500 CE which produced the central tenets of the Faith, including our canon, worship, creeds, and doctrine. TUMI is dedicated to helping urban churches retrieve these roots (also called the Great Tradition) for their spiritual renewal and missional vitality. For more information on Sacred Roots, visit www. tumi.org/sacredroots.*

This practical, helpful resource is especially designed to help new and growing Christians become effective disciples/warriors of Christ, and is built entirely on the Story of God as told in the Scriptures. Following the thematic outline of Ephesians, this lesson guide helps believers understand what the Bible says about the key dimensions of our participation in God's grand Story in nine integrated lessons. These studies lay out the key elements in how we fulfill our role in God's Story, allowing students to grow as disciples of Christ as they are grounded in the basics of the Christian faith and walk. This resource serves as our official precursor to TUMI's *Capstone Curriculum* seminary training, providing a solid introduction to the Bible's major themes as well as the foundational principles of Christian discipleship.

## Lesson Titles

Lesson 1: The Epic We Find Ourselves In:
        Joining Our Story with the Story of God

Lesson 2: The Enlistment We Make:
        Accepting Our Role in the Cosmic Conflict of the Ages

Lesson 3: The Entrance We Get:
        Linking Our Life with the Life of God in Christ

Lesson 4: The Endowment We Receive:
        The Holy Spirit's Role in the Good Fight of Faith

Lesson 5: The Excellence We Show:
        Living as Saints of God and Ambassadors of Christ in this World

Lesson 6: The Edification We Seek:
        Building up One Another in the Body of Christ

Lesson 7: The Enemy We Fight:
        Walking in Victory Against the Enemy of God

Lesson 8: The Equipment We Use:
        Putting on the Whole Armor of God

Lesson 9: The Endurance We Display:
        The Perseverance of the Saints

APPENDIX 13

## Standing Together for Christ
## Inside and Outside the Walls: The SIAFU Network

Rev. Dr. Don L. Davis • *www.tumi.org/siafu*

### Our Vision

At The Urban Ministry Institute (TUMI), we have a strong vision to equip men and women to return to society upon release from prison and jail. The best way to facilitate the process of reentry is to establish a network of friends and family who are ready to walk with men and women when they are released. This must be done the first hour, the first day, the first week, and the first month after they walk out the gate.

The second important factor is to create a strong sense of identity and belonging for men and women, while they are still incarcerated. Everyone needs to belong. SIAFU creates an identity for the incarcerated that can be carried forward when they are released. SIAFU chapters create a bridge of godly identity where the formerly incarcerated belong to something that transcends prison/jail.

### The SIAFU Network

SIAFU (pronouned *see-AH-foo*) is a practical means to enable urban disciples to stand together for Christ in the city!

### Mission Statement

SIAFU is a national association of Chapters anchored in local urban churches and ministries designed to identify, equip, and release spiritually qualified servant leaders to reach and transform the poorest unreached communities in urban America.

The link between incarceration and reentry can be served by local churches or ministries on the outside. Volunteers from these churches or organizations can sponsor and oversee SIAFU chapter gatherings functioning on the inside. And, after these prisoners have been released, the sponsoring church or ministry may welcome these ex-offenders into their chapter on the outside. We are convinced that these SIAFU sponsoring churches and ministries can provide long-term stability and service to institutions where rapid turnover occurs constantly, among inmate populations, chaplains, and officials.

### How SIAFU Chapters Work

We have designed an elegant, simple structure specifically designed to connect urban believers, both men and women, to come together, pray, fellowship, and challenge one another to fight for the sake of their churches, families, and communities. Chapters are hosted within local churches or related ministries. Since local churches are the outposts of the Kingdom, all SIAFU Chapters are connected to and under the authority of a local church or ministry.

APPENDIX 14
## *TUMI Satellite Network*
*www.tumi.org/satellite*

You can multiply disciples and develop leaders by starting a training center in your church, parachurch, prison, or denomination. As a TUMI satellite, you maintain your own identity and independence, while taking advantage of our curricula, administrative tools, and experience. You also join a network of other partner ministries who have similar aims, providing you with fellowship, support, and ideas. We provide each satellite with excellent and affordable theological resources so you can create your own training program that suits your ministry situation.

### Our Training Resources

The Urban Ministry Institute concentrates all of its educational programming on ministering effectively among city populations, and all of our classes are taught in light of the needs of urban ministry. We believe that the rapid growth of cities around the world presents both a challenge and an opportunity for the Church of Jesus Christ. The courses we offer are based on the Nicene Creed, which represents the essential core of our historic orthodox faith, affirmed through the Church's history.

*Fight the Good Fight of Faith* is a single-volume course that serves as our official precursor to TUMI's *Capstone Curriculum* seminary training, providing a solid introduction to the Bible's major themes as well as the foundational principles of Christian discipleship.

The *Capstone Curriculum* is a sixteen-module training program, taught at a seminary level, which we specifically designed to serve as the most essential knowledge and skill learning necessary for effective urban ministry and church leadership.

*Foundations for Ministry Series* courses are specially designed to help leaders grow in their knowledge of Scripture, theology, the Christian life, and practical ministry.

# The Evangel Network and the Evangel School of Urban Church Planting

www.tumi.org/churchplanting

## Planting Outposts of the Kingdom among the Lost

- Owning a vision to declare Christ as Lord and embody his victory in communities where he is not yet known.

- To collaborate and connect with like-minded people dedicated to leverage their resources to fulfill the Great Commission in the cities of America and around the world.

- Sharing resources and relationships to identify, equip, and release indigenous leaders to plant churches and launch new church planting movements.

## The Evangel School of Urban Church Planting

Our Evangel School of Urban Church Planting trains church planters to plant healthy churches among the city's poor, applying biblical wisdom in order to effectively evangelize, equip, and empower unreached city folk to respond to the love of Christ, and take their place in representing Christ's Kingdom where they live and work.

The Evangel School provides a tool for urban churches, denominations, and mission agencies to host a contextualized church plant school in their city or region for those God has called to plant churches among the urban poor.

The Evangel School Boot Camp includes a team assessment and an application process which helps to confirm that the planter has the calling, character, and competence required of a church planter working among the poor. Evangel Coaches come alongside the church planters and their teams to listen and cooperate with the Holy Spirit to see that their vision becomes a reality.

APPENDIX 16

# A Model of an Urban Church Association

Rev. Dr. Don L. Davis

**Affiliates** – those leaders and congregations who participate in association events and resources but retain their own autonomy and identity within another church community.

**Members** – those leaders and congregations who voluntarily submit to the authority and identity of the association for their growth and mission.

## Definition of observers, affiliates, and members.

1. Observers are allowed to attend select association events as friends of the association, with no further obligation to participate in its activities or initiatives.

2. Affiliates participate in sponsored association events, but do not sit or vote on its councils of authority. They associate voluntarily, that is, they retain their own authority and identity within their own church community. The connection they share with the association is based on shared values, resources, and mission.

3. Affiliates are not subject to decisions made by the association in regards to its doctrine, mission, and authority. They are limited to participate in those events, resource sharing, and mission projects allowed by the association.

4. Members voluntarily submit to the authority of the association, with full rights and privileges thereof, to contribute and represent it according to its protocols. Member churches are able to vote, be nominated for leadership, and participate in all levels of association business and mission.

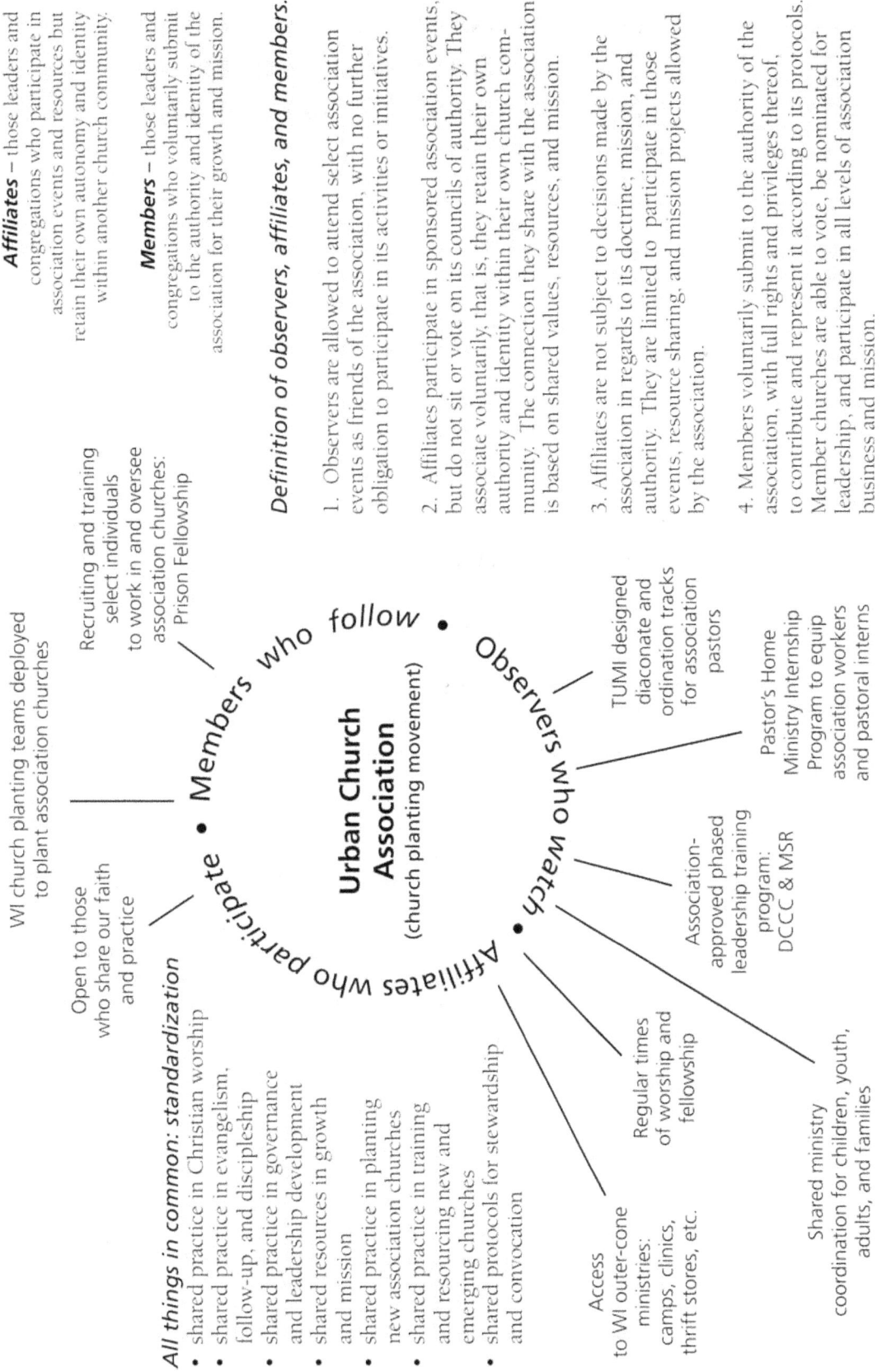

**Urban Church Association**
(church planting movement)

*Members who follow*

*Observers who watch*

*Affiliates who participate*

WI church planting teams deployed to plant association churches

Recruiting and training select individuals to work in and oversee association churches: Prison Fellowship

Open to those who share our faith and practice

*All things in common: standardization*
- shared practice in Christian worship
- shared practice in evangelism, follow-up, and discipleship
- shared practice in governance and leadership development
- shared resources in growth and mission
- shared practice in planting new association churches
- shared practice in training and resourcing new and emerging churches
- shared protocols for stewardship and convocation

Access to WI outer-cone ministries: camps, clinics, thrift stores, etc.

Regular times of worship and fellowship

Shared ministry coordination for children, youth, adults, and families

Association-approved phased leadership training program: DCCC & MSR

Pastor's Home Ministry Internship Program to equip association workers and pastoral interns

TUMI designed diaconate and ordination tracks for association pastors

APPENDIX 17

## *Let God Arise! Prayer Resources: Prayer for Spiritual Awakening and the Advancement of God's Kingdom*

*www.letgodarise.com*

*Let God Arise!* is a sober call to form aggressive movements of prayer for the city. We organize prayer asking God to break through the darkness, evil, and despair of the city, and that he might bring refreshment and revolutionary change among America's and the world's urban poor.

Prayer is the simple, elegant, and dynamic manner in which we accomplish the mission of God in the earth. As Jack Hayford said once, prayer is violence. It is violence against all things that oppose God, it treads down the darkness that enshrouds people's lives, and crushes the machinations of the rulers, the authorities, the cosmic powers of this present darkness, the spiritual forces of evil in the heavenly places (Eph. 6.12). Prayer is wrestling with these forces, not with fleshly strength, but with the truth and power of the Spirit. As Christians pray, they take up the armor of God, and bring down strongholds which interfere with the saving Gospel of Christ. Prayer ransacks the kingdom of darkness, it releases the captives, and allows the Lord to intervene and overcome the powers that oppress the city. Only God can win the day; only prayer can open the way.

We have designed numerous resources to help you, your small group, and your church to pray – for revival in jails and prisons, your city, country and beyond. Find the following information and links at *LetGodArise.com*:

- Resources for facilitating prayer concerts or groups
- Prayer ideas for your cities and the cities of the world
- Seasonal devotionals (video and pdf prayer guide)
- Tips on effective intercession
- Yearly prayer themes and resources including:
  - ~ *Biblical Revival*
  - ~ *The Battle Belongs to the Lord: Spiritual Warfare*
  - ~ *Like a Master Builder: The Foundation of Christ*
  - ~ *The Wondrous Cross*
  - ~ *The Good Shepherd*
  - ~ *The Just Shall Live by Faith*

Join us and the thousands of others who are interceding for the cities of the world!